WIDOW-WIDOWER'S HELPER

THERE IS HOPE!!!

What Do We Do After Our Mate Is Gone?

Resource, Remembrance and Restoration
Source Book
By Dr. Myrna L. Etheridge

authorHOUSE®

AuthorHouse™
1663 Liberty Drive
Bloomington, IN 47403
www.authorhouse.com
Phone: 1-800-839-8640

First published by AuthorHouse   09/27/2011

ISBN: 978-1-4670-4150-8 (sc)
ISBN: 978-1-4670-4483-7 (ebk)

These items were gathered as I lived going from where you are to where I am now. Our desire is you will be helped by this book.

Names and places within illustrations are fictitious or fabrications, except Grady's. This has been done to provide protection of true identities.

Unless otherwise identified, all Scripture quotations are from the New King James Version of the Bible. All emphases are added by the author.

Verses marked AMP are taken from the Amplified Bible, © The Lockman Foundation, 1954, 1958 (New Testament), © Zondervan Publishing House, 1962, 1964 (Old Testament).

Widow/Widower's Helper
© By Dr. Myrna L. Etheridge
2128 William #164
Cape Girardeau, Missouri 63801
www.gmeministries.org (Purchase downloadable or printed versions)

Cover Design By Diana DeBrock
Myrna L. Etheridge
September 2011
Cape Girardeau, Missouri USA
Printed in the USA For Worldwide Distribution
Library of Congress Registration Number:

Printed in the United States of America
This book is printed on acid-free paper.

DEDICATION

Without the inspiring lessons, laughter softened and awesome insights of thirty years this would never have been written. It is dedicated to the one who gave such a background for writing to help others as they deal with the ending of their remarkable story—ending their beautiful marriage.

In his departure this unique man gave courage to me to share with you and I now dedicate this work to Dr. Grady Lloyd Etheridge. He was a true Texan from an Oklahoma beginning. Most of all, he was my beloved husband for thirty years, 'ministerially' speaking—as Grady would have said. (I've said that since June 30th would have been our 30th anniversary. He went to his reward May 31!)

Friends have prodded and encouraged me to write to help others, since my complaints of "Where is the help for widows and widowers?" They have read, edited and sharpened the ideas, concepts and areas touched to bring help for you. Thank you to: Vivian Law, Agatha C. French, Carol Yates, David Roth and June Seabaugh for your variety of helps. Without them this probably wouldn't have come together.

TABLE OF CONTENTS

CHAPTER ONE

WOW! I DIDN'T THINK I
WOULD FEEL LIKE THIS!

Thinking is being pushed by the officials who seem to be in charge, taking that hunk of joy right out of my presence! Out of control to the MAX!

Then come all the questions: What funeral home will handle arrangements? What funeral, oh I have to decide that? What clothes will you want them to be dressed in? Which preacher/speaker will give the eulogy? What songs would be best? These are just a few asked of all of us at this time.

So many decisions and all while I'm crying internally but seem to be mute on the outside! The family may be about me, but I suddenly feel so very alone. What is happening to my world? Who needs to be called? What day will the funeral be? Where are my glasses—I'll need them to be able to see to call children, relatives, friends, clergy, etc.? Oh, they tell me to look on my head. This is probably going to be the longest day of my life—and the saddest.

The books from well-meaning people tell me that there are four phases to the mourning process—if I live that long! First, like I feel, there is the PAIN inside, the NUMBNESS of my feelings, the ANGER toward self, God, care givers, and my mate for leaving me! One dear widow put it, "Dar, how could you do this to me? I didn't tell you to go." These come and go at will. So do my tears!

Finally, they tell me—you'll COME TO TERMS with the loss and get on with life. Right now, you may not think you'll ever arrive at the place of coming to terms with the loss. The process takes time and it hurts terribly. (After almost two years I'm getting closer to this.) Let me assure you, I'm sorry for your loss—or I wouldn't be writing this expose of self trauma! All of this recounting of my personal loss is like screeching sound of nails going on a chalkboard!

For example, there is pain just dealing with the mail addressed to your mate. It is real! Get ready with a form to advise the maze of places and people who will send bills, sales information or inform your mate of something. You'll need the form so they can easily be told the change of residence and other appropriate information. You need to include a new address—or use an address label saying your mate's name and date of departure from this life. It took three trips to the bank to get the business office to remove his name and change the names on the checking account. I added another name besides my own so there are at least two names on the checking and bank accounts. I further complicated my changes by an address change at the same time. There was need for a place to physically mail things—but I was determined to no longer use my home as my mailing address.

Guess the number of calls you will have to endure to get through? Pray they are native English speaking people—the others? Well, I couldn't understand the comments. Finally, I learned we have a right to request that a state-side English speaking customer service representative speak with us! Do it. You have enough problems as it is!

Welcome to the group of people who knew this could happen, but never expected it—not really. Though you may say, "This isn't really happening!" It is! Trust me, it is happening. You will live again.

The widowers realize the clothes stay dirty until they wash them—or go to the laundry, if they know where it is. Meals do not jump on the table—even if you do feel hungry. Mostly you eat to stay alive—not stay alive to eat. Food often doesn't even taste good. You must eat to keep healthy. Change your diet to include healthy, green and red stuff. Yes, fruit and vegetables. Keep taking your vitamins, like your mate always told you! They are vitally important to your health. If you neglect your health at this time, you will probably be ill within the year. Check the statistics! Force yourself. Stay healthy. Cut down on animal source food and do the veggies, fruit and good carbohydrates. You know—be sensible—all things in moderation. Spend time in bed—even if sleep leaves you. Your body and heart need the down time. DO IT!

Shut the phone off if you think you can sleep because some insensitive person will call from across the country and get you up at 4 a.m. saying, "Oh my, is it really 4 a.m. there? It's 6 here." Such a friendship may not survive—even if you forgive easily! Afternoon naps? Yes, if you can. Rest allows your body to help you recover from the shock and stress of your loss.

Probably until after the visitation, first round of condolences and the funeral are over, you will not get much rest. If a family member or a friend can assist you during this time by driving you about and helping you keep on your time schedule, the stress will be less. Allow someone to help you.

The widows, from baby rearing days can still say, "Diapers get dirty! It happens!" Now this has happened—more awful to deal with but not as easily repairable as Huggies gone BAD! You will go through this. There is strength for each minute. Live them ONE at a TIME!

Welcome to the group of people who are once again where you didn't want to be: among the singles in your circle of married friends. Surprise, they probably do not want to deal with you. Be prepared to start a new group of friends—unless one or more of your friends are also single. For their own set of reasons they may have decided never to marry again. They probably will not voice the reasoning—just run from your presence!

Try not to be too surprised at anything, just smile. You'll find keeping a sense of humor helps almost all the time. The time it will not work is when your mate's longtime "probably old" friends want to see you crying and in the depth of mourning. Snuff, like you are crying, even if you are not, and say a teary "Thank you for your sympathy. We shall truly miss him/her." Then greet them—maybe with a hug, and let them cry. They probably will—even after your tears have all drained out. Reality has settled into your heart long ago. It could be years, far down the road of time. But, they didn't know—so mourning is NOW for them.

The loss of a mate is no one's cup of tea. They departed. We pray it was to the Lord Jesus' arms. Or if you are not into things of Jesus, ask strongly for mercy! Eternity, if we live so long in absence of peace and joyful activity, will be too long for words. And, I for one—do not want to be there without the hope as given in John 3:16.

"For God so loved the world that He gave His only begotten Son, that whosoever believeth on Him should not perish, but have everlasting life."

I do not want you to dwell on this. No matter the circumstance of a departure, they could have called out to the merciful Lord Jesus. He will respond to that type of choice of anyone who believes!

Eternity is without end. God is merciful, but belief in Jesus is a stated requirement of the truth filled, amazing story book, called the Bible.

The loss of a loved mate is settling into
Your favorite chair, warmed by your shawl, reading a great book,
Without the presence beside you of the one
Your heart loved.
Warmed by the fire, but you feel part of you is missing.

M. Etheridge's Widowhood Thoughts

The Loss of a Loved Mate
Is Facing the Bleakness of Winter
Without
The Joy from Colors of a Blazing Autumn.

M. Etheridge's Widowhood Thoughts

CHAPTER TWO

SITTING ALONE—EVEN WITHIN THE FAMILY?
WHAT HAPPENS NEXT?

Planning for the funeral comes next after the family arrives. Probably some family member will want to write, or if there has been prolonged illness—they will have written at least part of what could be used during the eulogy. Sometimes several persons may be asked to participate in the memorial service.

Usually, there is a family leader who helps with selection of the—look and garments for the last public appearance, if your family does them. Some say goodbye at the time of death and not again. Whatever your composite family's tradition is will probably take away all but the strongest of your mate's voiced demands.

Usually, we're just too numb to protest strongly. If you had completed durable power of attorney forms your mate's personal choices were done, so rest in that fact. Selection of pre-need burial items is a total blessing at this time. If your mate was wise and did this for you, be very thankful!

The pre-need paid burials can be transferred from where the arrangements were made to another funeral home. If you need a funeral home closer to where you are now, ASK for that service. Let it be known and insist upon your need being met. There could even be an itemized list of your mate's desires for music, minister, etc. The funeral home will have a copy of the pre-need information even if you can't find the paper work at home.

The funeral home will ask about:

> Birth certificate with Mate's birth place
> Marriage certificate,
> Burial lot Owners Deed
> Insurance Policy
> If there is a proper will
> Bible or listing of parents, siblings, children
> Obituary for the papers/radio announcements (Some news- papers charge for printing the notice, your funeral director will help your announcement length keep within the allowed limit—to help you keep the fees reasonable.)
> Funeral (The parts: viewing-visitation, service time, as to content of the service, minister, music, etc.—your decisions are the calls that they follow.)
> Number of Death Certificates to order (6 probably)

Ideally, all this information was stored together. If not, you will need to locate these items. Sorry, but you will need to find this type of information within a day or so of the death of your mate. Get to the bank and empty the safe deposit box as soon as possible and get some cash money from your checking account in case these become temporarily closed to you. Take what you need with you to the funeral home if possible.

Let me suggest that if you own real property—like a home—order 6 death certificates. Some places will take copies, but get six when the funeral director asks. If you operate a business you might need more. They are about $10.00 a copy.

For example: Social Security will request lots of information. All you will need for them is listed with the paper work part of this book on pages 37 through 51.

To give you an idea of these requests, in brief: Social Security wants a copy of the Death Certificate before they will change your benefit amount to a widow's status. To avoid multiple trips to the various offices and to the Social Security office go armed with the list of parents, etc. They'll ask for your marriage license and even the marriage date when he married his long deceased first wife! (A widow may request to draw benefits from a former husband of eleven years or more of marriage—if the benefits are better. It doesn't affect the former husband's benefits at all.) Many businesses, like your bank, want a copy of the Death Certificate, or to see and then copy the original for their records before they will change your accounts.

Probably the papers you need are in a home safe or file. If not, check the Bank Safety Deposit Box (If death is expected, wisdom is do this before death.) as soon as possible after death to get the contents out. It may be legally locked if you do not.

Try to work on these items along with the choices and arrangements for the funeral. Remember, the power of love and the prayers of your friends will be supporting all you to do at this time. God is faithful and will strengthen your body and mind.

Make a list of people to be contacted. Allow others to help with the calls, emails, etc., to contact as many persons as you feel is necessary.

Sometimes there are time crunches because the church, funeral home or other professional venue has other arrangements that have been previously made. Our church was busy for the two days we ideally needed to use it. The meeting had been scheduled for a long time. We tried to make do with the available days.

The result was we couldn't contact as many persons living at distances as we desired. Some later shared they were unable to attend.

Yet, pastor, knowing my funds were very limited, called several persons who had looked to my husband as a father/mentor in the ministry to help by giving money instead of floral arrangements. Quickly the funeral costs were taken care of by their provisions. Others will help you meet the needs when you can't do it alone! Express your needs so their love may support you at this time. It's not being greedy—it is need. Have someone help you and keep good records of gifts so you can send thank you notes in a timely manner. Before going to the funeral home for arrangements—if they were not already made—be aware the funeral director will show you all the various types of caskets. The most reasonable will be the last one after you refuse all the others! It will probably be just like one you've already seen, but the cost will be far more reasonable.

Remember the concrete vault works just as well as stainless steel. The cost is far less! Yes, it costs for the burial plot and to open the grave. In some areas the cost of this land is considerable! Gather the clothes and jewelry. (Rings and other items

7

displayed on your loved one are best kept by the family, but often some leave something special. Do as you like. It's your loved one's funeral.)

Determine the type of service and tell the funeral director what you want done. The lid can be up or down—that's your choice. There can be a last viewing or not. That's your choice too. Do what you can deal with. Be considerate of yourself!

Even the gifts to ministers or musicians are at your discretion. Dr. Grady ministered for 69 years and the largest offering for a funeral was when he prayed over the remains of a favorite dog. The dog was so loved that when Grady prayed a beautiful prayer over "the faithful friend and companion" we all cried. I really was amazed at the $100.00 honorarium! Usually it is $50.00, but you could give any offering you can afford. Ask your funeral director, if you like. The minister who comes two or three times to the funeral home and travels to the graveside has a considerable investment of time and expense. They will appreciate any gift. My experience was that each of the three gifts of $100.00 and one of $50.00 returned—one way or another.

My husband's only child was so very upset by his passing that she didn't come to the funeral from her distant home. It was ok. That was her right and what she could do. And, her "My Pop" writing won the hearts of all who read it. Her love was there. We missed her, but I totally understood. We agreed on the spray for the casket and I ordered it from the local florist. We marked it "Husband" and "Pop." Family members did an "Uncle" arrangement on a heart. There were plenty of floral arrangements in addition to the money gifts. During the thirty years of ministry and far more of life, all the funerals have had ample show of the love and generosity of friends in beautiful flowers!

We decided to have a church viewing after the funeral service at my church, in another town. Many in that church looked to my mate as their beloved Pastor. (He spent 69 years in ministry. Eight were with this congregation.) The power point presentation of pictures of Dr. Grady's life gave a testimony and included many memories from this second church group. The electronics were a bit of a challenge, but it was worth the effort. The people who loved him came—many of the aged were most grateful that we chose to come to them.

The interment the next day was for immediate family, closest friends and my Pastors. We sang, "When We All Get to Heaven." We all cried with joy for he kept the faith. My "Baby" was faithful to God's call for all his 86 years! Make sure your mate's funeral is a final masterpiece.

Decisions on the grave marker can be done later. Dr. Grady served in the Marines and was eligible for the gift military marker. His daughter took care of the setting costs and arrangements for me. The marker is very nicely done. The bronze is like he was, durable and beautiful.

What do you do when you, the surviving mate, can't remember some of the particulars—and only you can make the decision? PRAY! PRAY! PRAY! When you have peace about a choice? YES, JUST DO IT! No choice is wrong, just unique to you.

The Widower reflects:

This is the first Super Bowl that I have been able to watch without having a "honey do" request during the fourth quarter. Just think, the quarter back is running for the touchdown that will tie up the score and I can watch!
(Must have been a woman thing.)

M. Etheridge's Widowhood Thoughts

ABOUT THE AUTHOR Myrna L. Etheridge

Here are some of the reasons she would write this book:
Mother of two deceased sons
Widow of one deceased husband
Divorcee with no living children, so no communication avenues
Both parents are deceased
Eldest of four children
Two siblings; brother Louis and sister Margaret, deceased
(Many friends and classmates are too)
Formerly Cystic Fibrosis symptoms, with severe learning disability until age 41,
Ill until 41 with infections and allergies
College undergraduate degree took nine years to accomplish—so went on to BSE
        Biology; MSE Biology Education; Ph.D. emphasis in
        Systematic Theology, and D.D. honors
Authoress or contributing Editor for fourteen other books
Music CD, To Your Glory Lord, with 8 of her original songs-Piano music and vocal
        (her voice and piano playing)
Spent youth years as part of a working farm family drove tractor by age ten
Born again gloriously, at age nine
Called at 12, "Will you go where I tell you?" Answer: "Yes!"

She just had to share what her husband of thirty years' Dr. Grady's death has taught her. She has endured every type of loss and is writing for your benefit.

CHAPTER THREE

HOW DO I DRESS? WHAT SHOULD I DO?

Pleasant thoughts of at least one very happy memory will help you when the first viewing time arrives. Make sure you have some support. Emotions tend to surprise even the most stern widows and widowers. The true mortician is an artist! They'll look so much better than your last look at them at time of death. Don't worry.

Select your clothes thinking about matching your mate like you've done for years. Be you. Dress well like you were going to an important meeting.

As a widow, I wore a hat—mainly because no one could see me really well and besides that they had to keep a distance from the brim. (They didn't know that.) Additionally, my hair was not in great shape after the ordeal of the loss of sleep and the physical stress of the wind down of life for a beloved husband.

Oh yes, bathe. Remember deodorant. And, wear shoes that are mildly dressy as well as comfortable for the viewing time and for the funeral. No sense having pain in your feet as well as having pain of loss and your broken heart.

People always want details, but you are not obliged to give them. Be you. When you feel stressed, go to the restroom; get a drink of water or juice. Sit on the front pew and allow people to come to you. The ones who loved your mate will want to tell you why they were special. Pretend to listen and often you will learn of some great, encouraging happenings. Even if you just weep while you listen, it will be well tolerated and understood at this time.

It is best to choose not to be angry with your mate that there was little or no planning for this time. Even worse is when a funeral was one of the "Do not go there!" topics. Now you are forced to go there—for there is no choice! You have to make the decisions. The pre-need planning would have been far more humane.

Think deeply about what you wear starting today. Answer the question: "What are you trying to say about who you are?" Dress like a character out of the trilogy of the "Ring" and "walla" the wrong people are alerted to pay attention to you. Dress like an 1890's southern belle and you will become overly concerned with beauty shop appointments. You may have a jumping major trauma when you can't get a properly done nail job or have your golf clubs cleaned and waxed just so! This is not meaning to say we never need to have beauty shop appointments or have great golf services. But, they must not be the basis of your self-identification. Especially not for this event!

Talk with yourself. Who are you? Did you make major changes to please your mate and keep peace in your household?

Now, however, that is not who you are. Begin to find out who you really are because the "Real YOU" may now step forward! You are free to do this! Please, find out who you are.

Explain to yourself about you and begin to change your manner of dress to suit the real you. You will find that folks expect you to wear black or dark "mourning" clothing for six months to a year. Personally my choice was to begin adding colored jackets to black skirt and tops or darker colors about six weeks after my husband was gone. Occasionally, after about six months, other outfits in modest and conservative colors were added. My husband was so well known that I did not choose to go too quickly through the outward mourning.

I couldn't do the inward grieving quickly either. After one year had passed I stopped wearing lots of dark colors. Mourning is a process each person must pass through often with a day now and then watered with lots of tears.

Each of you will need to work through your own grief process. Consider the record of my choices as a point of reference, but be yourself.

Widowers often find the mourning far more painful than the widows. The "men don't cry" thing is a false idea. Men hurt and crying is a safety valve. Men, use your mourning time to get well. Carry the pain internally and you will take far longer to heal. A quick marriage will not take away the mourning process. You may not even remember the first two years of a quick after death of wife marriage!

My husband did not remember most of what happened during the first two years of our marriage. His wife of 33 years died and we were married six months later. He had few memories of the first two years of our marriage. As the wife—that hurt! His daughter had a terrible adjustment time too. It was painful for all three of us, but we did recover and 30 years later we're dealing and helping each other nicely with the grief of his loss.

Any major change within two years of the time of your loss is dangerous! Probably it will be a poor or terrible choice. Do not make major decisions unless you have no choice. Internalize this truth!

Children sometimes act like both of you died! Do not allow the children to take all your furniture, "all Mom's things" or "all Dad's things" from your home. You are still living. Remind them and try to help them mourn too. Mourning is a natural process. It doesn't mean you haven't hope of eternity—it means you miss a loved one!

They have a painful loss too. Cry together. Avoid saying, "God wanted her more than we did." That's probably a lie!

God didn't want Dad or Mom more than you do! Please, don't make God the bad guy. Bad things happen to good people. We often have no clue why they happened—so give God a break! The whys are usually not understood. Just hurt and ask God to comfort you in your loss.

The LORD has been mindful of us: He will bless us . . . He will bless those who reverently and worshipfully fear the LORD, both small and great . . . The dead praise not the LORD, neither any that go down into silence. But we will bless—affectionately and gratefully praise—the LORD from this time forth and forever. Praise the Lord! Hallelujah!
Psalms 115:12-13, 17-18 AMP

Do your best to continue with the mail as it comes in. Balance the check book/s and find out where all the business papers are. If there isn't a file with some semblance of order, make one. Try to establish some controllable records so you do not overdraft the check book during this very stress-filled week and time.

Social Security will back draft the last check paid to any person drawing it. Yes, they will! My mother's check book was over drafted because of that and mine would have been too, but I went in to talk with the Social Security customer service representative very soon—without the Death Certificate. They told me it would be back drafted for the whole month! Then I had to go back. They had told me all the things I needed to know or bring. You'll find them listed in the paper chapter.

Money is often an area where one mate had little or no knowledge of the family status. Remember the "we don't talk about that" area of the investments? Now you have to take care of it. Call the CPA, lawyer or a smart, close-mouthed friend. After you have received advice from several persons make the decisions. Remember if you delay a decision long enough it will make its own choice, and you will probably not like what it is. Make a decision. Go on, you can do it.

The address changes

The vitamin company decided live people purchase more vitamins than the others do long distance (from Heaven).
They only required one notice!

M. Etheridge's Widowhood Thoughts

CHAPTER FOUR

HOW DO I COPE? WHAT'S NEXT?

Devotion to God can become so vital that His presence melts your soul with
His type of fire. It will burn away selfishness and you'll find
New joy living for the benefit of others.

M. Etheridge's Widowhood Thoughts

Each day after the visiting family and friends return to their lives you have the everyday things to tend to. For widows the laundry, housekeeping, cooking and errands are old hat. Perhaps you do not want to do them, but force yourself. Comfort comes more quickly when you return to some sort of routine.

Widowers may become even more overwhelmed than widows when the laundry is still dirty. Then they find their shirt or slacks or whatever are still in the same place they left them and are not ready for use. Not to mention that the daily household tasks and cooking aren't happening. They hadn't thought of these for years—or maybe never did! (Think about a "butler?")

Yet, maybe they are not as over whelmed as a woman whose husband was admitted to a local nursing home. This eighty-five year old requested her son come to her home. She told him she needed some help. He went.

"Mom, what do you need?

"Son, will you go with me to buy gasoline for the car?"

The son was totally flustered. His mother was a resourceful and intelligent woman. "Mom, it's totally easy to do."

"In all these 65 years of marriage your Dad always filled the gas tank and took care of the auto. I don't know what to do." Her honest reply stunned her son.

"O. K. Mom, let's go. It's easy. I'll help you this time." They went. He did. She learned and filled that gas tank for another four years before she stopped driving.

****

For me the most stressful time was when I needed to face the following situation.

Widowhood is
Having cold feet—knowing
No one shouts "stop that!" when I stretch
Out my legs seeking some warmth.
There's no response! There's no help!

M. Etheridge's Widowhood Thoughts

Each of you reading this will have similar thoughts run through your mind.

Being single is a shock. We might have thought it could happen, but now it is our life. The shock is real!

We may find a knee slapping story
That's really funny—but just a bit
On the "rare side"—with
No one with whom we can safely share it.

M. Etheridge's Widowhood Thoughts

Each day has, or can have tasks, so the best thing we can do is determine our plan. We will, bit by bit, work through the paper chase of our mate's passing.

My Dad told my mother that she didn't need to do anything after he went home to heaven. "The kids can take care of it." She didn't either!

When she died it took a court hearing to get that mess they made righted. When I was asked by the lawyer why my Mother hadn't taken my Dad's estate through Probate I had to answer, "My Mom and Dad were married for forty-four years and he traveled doing his work. I suppose she just pretended he was gone on a trip so she didn't have to face his death, or do anything, because he'd be home soon."

They loved each other dearly and enjoyed a happy marriage. I was in charge of the disbursements of their household goods. The will was one my Dad did. And the judge didn't like that either, but we worked through it without incident. (The legal guys were amazed we did.)

First thing the funeral director will ask you is "How many Thank You notes you will need?" Be greedy. Even if you have some left over—get a generous amount. (An extra box full probably should be returned to the funeral home.) Remember the Ministers and Musicians with the first ones you write so you have them prepared for the funeral director to give to the ones you've asked to help. These notes are specially worded and are difficult to find anywhere besides the one place you really do not want to go back to—the funeral home! Get busy. At least address the others soon after the funeral!

You think you will remember, but probably you will not accurately remember. You have just had shock therapy. It was—a funeral for your honey, baby, darling, bride, sweetheart, sugar daddy—or whatever term of endearment you used.

(There will be other trips to "it"—by someone.) First, the trip back to pick up Certificates, next to provide the insurance papers, or pay the bill—or make arrangements for paying it. Sorry, you will not be able to avoid "IT" (the funeral home) completely. Your loved one is placed at rest and they helped you. So, be thankful—no matter what happened.

Determine a spot in the home—that doesn't have too many memories to use for doing paper work. This is so you can concentrate—even if tears pour out like glasses-full of water would.

The weeping may continue when you write the Thank You notes. Next paper work will be the changes of address/name/or whatever you need.

It will be months—perhaps over a year—before all the paper stuff is completed. Do it one at a time! No one can do it all at once! (I still have the title to the home to be changed from our names to my name. There are some title change fees and a lawyer needed—so it has to wait a bit longer. You may have something like that too.)

Find a notebook or better—so you don't lose the pages—a spiral bound notebook. Get your scotch tape, a pen and some paper clips gathered together with the incoming mail and gather the bills from the place where they land. (You know—the 'that's where they land' area. Almost everybody has a place like that.)

Get some return address labels. (Find the kind you have hundreds of after you helped the disabled American Veterans ONCE.) Make some address labels with your computer and printer along with another return address label that says something similar to the following.

Notice that the date of death and address changes are both mentioned. All I needed to do was paste it into a letter telling the company to change, remove or whatever was needed.

> Grady Etheridge deceased 5/31/09.
> Remove from your files please.
> From: PO Box 564, Sikeston, MO 63801
> TO: 2128 William #164, Cape Girardeau, MO 63703

If you don't have any of these, ask your kids or neighbor to do some for you. Then photocopy one page and print them on plain paper. (You can cut and scotch tape them onto the letters for address change labels.) The post office has change of address post cards. Buy postage for the post cards while you are there. And get a

18

couple of sets. Make a list of the ones you send out. Do it! (Some I did three times to get them to be updated.)

Some businesses required that you and anyone whose name you are adding visit their office to make any change in names on their accounts. You will need to wait until after the Death Certificates arrive back to the funeral home before you can change most items. We'll explore this later.

Take the communications and then begin to write each item or company name on the top of a page in your spiral notebook. You'll want a tab of scotch tape with a hint at the name so you can find that page more easily. Even if you start in alphabetical order, they get mixed up before all the items are listed.

FOR EXAMPLE:
The first one I chose to write down was Du Bail Judge. (They are my legal protection provider. Your lawyer will help you with this.) What I wanted to know or do were:

- What was needed to get my will updated?
- How to remove my Spouse's name from this legal service's membership?
- Register my new address with them
- What do I do with my spouses' will? What about Probate Court?

DuBail told me after three calls—what to do in Missouri: (Each state has legal differences, so ASK! Some states change requirements by counties.) This is repeated later for emphasis.

1) Do a new will (They sent the form for me to fill in.) Next when they sent the formal will I had to have it witnessed, certified and make two copies of it. They advise keeping the original in a safe or secured location.
2) Call a lawyer in Cape to find out about the Probate Court in my area. (I found out the name of the secretary from a lawyer friend.)
3) Go to Probate Court and it requires that the: Will and Death Certificate be taken to the County Probate Division in Cape Girardeau at the Old Court House, in the office on Lorimar and to answer the following questions:
   a. Present to Probate: Will and Death Certificate (6/27/09 presented) Be prepared to pay a small fee.
   b. File will—no assets (Telling them there are no assets—no property listed only in your spouses' name)

19

      c.   State (SAY) to them: "Probate does not need to 'open this will'." (If both names are **not** on real property you will need to "open the will.")

      d.   When you have no children to inherit your things—to keep assets out of probate you may:

          i.   Do a Title on Death "TOD" or a

          ii. Beneficiary Deed to your assets

4)   Collect a receipt for the recording of the will (They sent it back 7/9/09). File the receipt with your spouse's permanent records and a copy of the presented will. Yes, do a file.

This first one is VERY IMPORTANT! DO IT! (The TOD I placed on my **paid off** automobile title was done when I changed the title ownership to me and my sister's names. So, at my death—no sweat! The auto will automatically be hers, **Title On Death**. (I do not desire more probate hearings after the fact if it can be easily avoided!)

I couldn't do this with my real property, because it is **not debt free** as of this time. If I did, the other option, Beneficiary Deed, she would have to PAY OFF the loan immediately upon my death. Not good for her! So, she'll have to deal with the property after I'm deceased.

As you work though all of these items **keep** the

      1)   Names of people who work with you
      2)   Phone numbers of key persons and the
      3)   Specific things you are to do **written down**.

Then, since the stress level is so high, if/when you forget you can be easily reminded of the process thus far. (Notice: The probate took from death May 31 to filing June 7 to July 5, '09 to get the receipt back to me.)

There are several other important tasks that we will cover **in detail** like this. This book is being written so you will have the benefit of what my loss caused me to learn—the hard way.

Right now I remember that Widowhood is
Sitting alone, crying in sympathy
With "Anne of Green Gables" but no one hands me a hankie.

M. Etheridge's Widowhood Thoughts

<u>YET REMEMBER and THIS IS IMPORTANT:</u>

Creating a Masterpiece Of Memories Is like leaving a
Treasure to your Family. They are paintings
In colors Of Love!

M. Etheridge's Widowhood Thoughts

Then he is Amazed and-The Widower reflects:

This is the first Baseball Playoffs that I have been able to watch
Without having to explain what a batting average means.

And, even in a twelve inning game—nothing else needed to be done, fixed or
taken care or answered. and I can shout all I want
Without a "What's happened now?" alarmed response from the kitchen!

(Must have been a woman thing?)
M. Etheridge's Widowhood Thoughts

21

CHAPTER FIVE

THE MAIL IS HERE!
SYMPATHY CONTINUES

Determination will overcome the mail and name changes!

Do not faint. Be patient. Make it a game. Be diligent. Cry when necessary, but persevere!

His college training institution took six months to get his name into their 'obits.' They finally did a beautiful piece on his remarkable life in the monthly magazine. But OH MY, six months! They finally knew he was home in Heaven.

> *Since they assumed his widow might just have some memorial*
> *Money—they added mine with the correct address change!*
> *Boy, were they wrong about the money!*
>
> *M. Etheridge's Widowhood Thought.*

Ever ask yourself, "What response did I get to 'What do I do if some things happen and you can't take care of that item?'" (That's usually in a "whatever we weren't allowed to do or ask about" area.)

As the remaining mate, pray for wisdom and courage. Then ACT when you have peace about the tentative decision. Remember, God guides the steps of a righteous person! This kind of peace is past understanding. You just feel O.K. about the choice.

If it is a really bad choice, you will know soon enough. So relax. A successful executive is anyone who is right 51% of the time! (I know, we want to be 100% right—but get real—that's not like real life.)

Meanwhile handle the mail as it comes. This will give you a task for the day besides work, if you are still employed and keeping a schedule. If you are not, it will give you a reason to get up, take care of your body and prepare for the day.

Try to change any ritual you used to have with your mate for the wake up times. This will develop a new pattern for your life—if you want to change it. If not—you will have more challenges since most of the next few months will always involve changes from what was and "what we used to do" activities.

As an example: For thirty years of married life, each morning I listened to a ten to fifteen minute Bible expounding sermon done by my husband.

At first I thought it was to be a conversation, but quickly learned he wanted to be heard—not conversed with! So the private sermons continued for all our married life. He never wanted to change and I didn't try to change him.

However, I did want God to talk with me in the morning. For years I got up one to three hours earlier than my spouse to have the luxury of listening to my Maker first. Later each morning, I listened to a very learned, excellent preacher for the Word of the Day—the soliloquy. That's what I called it, but was it just for me—or, for the world? I never really knew. I did know that NO RESPONSE was desired. After a couple of lame tries—I quit! Still much information was stowed away during each soliloquy. I listened intently to gain the drops of Bible wisdom. Dr. Grady was a rare find of humor bound with wisdom.

Remember the special understandings you had with your mate. They formed much of the framework that kept you together during your marriage. Value these kinds of memories.

What will I do each morning now? My decision was to enhance the meeting with my Maker. I constructed a kneeling cushion and found a short table to use as the altar. A dear friend helped me attach the cushion to the little frame—like an upholstery piece. It is in my upstairs mail office.

It used to be Dr. Grady's office. At first I cried almost each time I went there to work on the mail and other business changes. Now, almost two years later, I have the altar and have moved the desk arrangement to a different location—my choice.

Even today I spent prayer time and enjoyed thinking about the growth all the changes have prompted in me. I also often do calls and note writing there—now usually without tears.

Decisions like what to do with things and clothing of your loved one need to be pushed away until after the funeral is over and they send or you have picked up the Death Certificates.

Allow ten days to two weeks and insist that your family allow you the luxury of that time to settle down inside. Then determine how to handle the personal items. Children may want to help, but you need to list where items end up. Because you think you will remember, but most likely—you will not recollect what was done with some item at a later time. The stress level is still very high.

After the funeral and time had passed, I started forcing myself to make some of the choices.

There were family heirlooms that my husband had held. I listed the ones to be sent to his daughter. Within the first month I packed them and shipped the most important ones to her. Later a three generation book case (HEAVY) was taken with help from my children in the Lord, to a nearby relative. This meant all that belonged to Dr. Grady's first wife's family were with proper family members. This freed me up to disperse useful items to persons who loved him or requested something to 'remember him by.'

I kept only a few items of his personal things: a house coat, a tee shirt and a couple of pieces of jewelry. Yes, I kept sermons, notes and study Bibles and books he used the most. These make up my memory keepsakes to hug and remember good times.

His clothes are not hanging in the closet to haunt me. These types of items can be given, discarded, resold or recycled. Don't hurt yourself by having your mate's clothes in the closet for months or years. Please, they will not be back. That's sad but true.

Use various means to disperse all the goods. The hearing aid center that served my man well received his nearly new hearing aids. They have a company that will refit them for a person who has financial limitations and hearing problems.

Others get stuck in mourning. That is not a good place to stall. I suggest Bible study and meeting with a local support group for anyone continuing to have strong mourning. Maybe one or two visits to graveside are normal. But, if you are going each day and crying the rest of the day—get some help. Your physical being will soon be affected as well and may be pushing you toward a depression. (Later, we'll talk about your health and clothing in detail.)

Again, focus on the mail. If the business items are not handled your life can become a small nightmare! Some will blame their mate for the confusion. Others seek to find some social setting to "forget the sorrow."

Please yourself and some of your relatives as to how someone in your situation would best behave. Wild parties or even social gatherings can crash on your emotions like a huge wave! Emotions need healing before you benefit from or normally react to social interactions. Your emotions have been stressed. Probably, you will neither enjoy nor need gala events for some time. Go slow with small group exchanges. You may find—though others don't—that a certain topic ends up with a flood of tears for you. Maybe it was a rage? Do not make apologies. We all hurt when a loved one leaves.

If persons don't understand or know you, say something like, "I thought I was ready for some socialization, but I'm not." Excuse yourself and LEAVE the gathering if at all possible.

Special friends of both you and your departed will be of most assistance in helping you get through the angers—hurts and frustrations generated by spousal failures. If they loved both of you they will hear you—comment and maybe agree. But they will not repeat what you've shared with them. That's very good, since you could hear gossip for years if you shared at this depth with anyone who doesn't love both of you!

When your emotions are raw, and they will be from time to time—stay home, rent a comforting movie, or write address change letters, you know, the ones that are waiting to be posted.

Grab that spiral notebook and write the address changes at the back from the outside in. I didn't do this. The pieces of papers—they became quite a stack—have escaped from me! Last week (one and a half years into this) I wrote three more letters to update the address and mail name! Wonder if it will ever be over? Prepare for the long haul!

Have a great announcement for you. My city utility company has decided I pay the bills and transferred the deposit name to Myrna Etheridge! It only took a year and four months to get this done. Finally, in the local office I begged. They changed it for me. In a time of mercy, one city employee did the miraculous—changed an account owners' name. I danced all the way to my parked auto!

The comical part of this is the state wide electric and natural gas provider WILL NOT CHANGE THE NAME of the one who opened the account—no matter if you pay the bill or not. Only way to change it is start up a new account at your home address! I don't think so—shut off the gas and electricity to restart it with a new deposit before the old one comes back? No, not going there! I just continue to write Mrs. before my sweetie's name each month. It has been almost two years and I pay the bills on time—so the service continues.

At least I do not have to wash the auto when I don't want to!

Widowhood is Being able to drive your auto when it really needs to be washed—without expecting a rebuff for the yucky auto!
Who cares anyway?
You'd think it was a husband's face that was dirty.
Right? (Must be a man thing.)

M. Etheridge's Widowhood Thought

CHAPTER SIX

THE TEARS,
WHEN WILL THEY STOP POPPING OUT?

My nephew-in-law is a wonderful doctor. He keeps my smile pretty and I'm most thankful for his professional help. After the appointment they graciously opened their home for an overnight visit. We laughed over dinner and I retired to the special guest bedroom.

Everywhere I looked the past stared back at me.

The last doll my parents got for my Christmas as a 12 year old is there on the bed needing me to make her a new dress. (I started dressing dolls at age nine, so I thought this would be simple.) It has been ten months since my spouse's home-going. I thought I was doing well, but here I sit on the bed inwardly sobbing! I'm measuring the doll all right, and holding back sobs. I enjoyed my doll so very much and the last dress was one my sister, sixteen months my junior made. It was a lovely Queen Anne outfit new in 1955. Now, I'm measuring it for a new dress. (The trauma was such that it isn't finished yet—a year later.)

Looking about this room I realize I'm resting among memories of my beloved family. From the dresser my Mother stared with a smile captured after she knew she was dying. My departed sister, who was like my twin, was there standing beside me (my thirty-five year old self) and my youngest sister flanked me on the left. It was the only time we, three adult women had our portrait made. I'm now ashamed of the woman I was at that time in my life. I began sniffing even more.

The furniture represented four generations of my family and called other history to my remembrance. The mahogany burl front wardrobe from France circa 1850's is still so beautiful. We truly loved one another. We have been a devoted family for a long time. The tears rolled involuntarily down my cheeks as I completed the measurements for dolly's new dress.

THE FUNERAL IS OVER!

Think about your situation. No one will clean house for us or cause us to exercise. Why do I care? (You'll get good at talking to yourself! Be positive and exercise authority over bad attitudes.) If you feel sorry for yourself when you face reality, have SHORT PITTY PARTIES, then laugh at yourself!

Since the ending of a life is now laid to rest, you will need to get settled in to take care of the rest of yours. First there are the final paper work items for your mate and you. These include making certain your needed items are put into order for the one/s that will take care of a funeral for you.

Next for you personally there are three more. EXERCISE, DIET and maintaining your HOME. These are keys to maintaining your health.

A woman's home tells about her mental health. What does yours tell about you? Do not laugh, men! A man's auto tells about his mental health. What does yours tell about you? A chapter on each of these follows. My cleaning chart is there too.

Even with my house cleaning chart,
I don't always choose to follow it.
That's my decision too.

The choices made at this time
Put me into a position of rest,
And generate a sense of well being.
When my life is in order
And under the direction of the LORD God,
Creator of the Universe, peace will surround me.

M. Etheridge's Widowhood Thought

CHAPTER SEVEN

THE TRUTH FACTORS

A new type of liberty has come to you. You can determine freely and be responsible for, your own words and actions. Your mate will not descend upon your words or actions with adamant disapproval or censures. No, "I'm not talking to you after that action!" sentences will be passed upon you. Relax. The funeral is over. The family has gone home and you are on your own—plus your family responsibilities. You are single before God! Additionally there is that scripture that gives me deep conviction of well-being.

I can do all things through Christ,
(THIS TRUTH GIVES ME ENERGY FOR TODAY)
which strengtheneth me.
Philippians 4:13

Widowhood in retirement years
Is being able to wait until noontime to get dressed. With or without
Makeup applied there are no comments.
You can be yourself!
Do makeup—if you want to! No pressure.
Just please yourself.

M. Etheridge's Widowhood thoughts

Widowhood is deciding when you want to take off your wedding band or diamond.
Take your time! If you were a loved mate—you will wait until you are ready.
If he was a cheat or didn't really love you, wear it when you travel.
That keeps down the hassles and says a man/woman may be nearby.

M. Etheridge's Widowhood Thoughts

You can say it as you see it. What you desire to report is without a "Why did you say that?"

Widowhood is:
Being able to be honest about your husband's
Mother's cooking, her character, her
Housekeeping anytime you want to do it.
(Yeah! She's no longer perfect.
I always knew I wasn't.)

M. Etheridge's Widowhood Thoughts

The Truth about—
Revealing Myrna's House Task List.

My growing up time was filled with Obsessive-Compulsive cleaning habits. My mother never had to do anything but dust mop her hardwood floors until after I married at nineteen.

This compulsion for cleanliness continued until about age twenty-eight when I hired a house cleaning agency to do my home in Puerto Rico. Their pattern of cleaning—which was excellent influenced this list.

This schedule was formally designed for a corporate office complex. I was responsible for maintaining it. And, I've used it since then.

No, not religiously every Monday and Thursday, but to "keep my home in order and clean enough to be healthy and dirty enough to be lived in." (That less than perfect motto was one I didn't like for years.)

I thought of it as slovenly, but my youthful compulsions have given way to a no-nonsense, six hours a week plan. Now I have a livable, clean, and orderly home. Everything has a place—even the book stock and it is in its place now.

You can use this schedule to tell your maid or cleaning service what you want done! NO HASSELS! Copy this list and walla, you have orders for cleaning your home! From stem to stern each four months of the year even the once a year things are included. If your home layout is different, modify it, but it works.

The schedule is by the week of the month. Just check which week of the month it is and begin to set your home in a clean and working order. It will work no matter what yours looks like now!

> *Happiness is having a house that is clean and in place*
> *Even when the world happens to come by for a quick visit.*
>
> *M. Etheridge's Widowhood Thoughts*

HOUSE KEEPING CLEANING SCHEDULE

CLEANING TASK/DAYS	MONDAYS (3 HRS)	THURSDAYS (3 HRS)
WEEK #1	Kitchen/Gen.Clean	Bed Room Dusting
`	Clean Refrigerator	Change Bed Linens
	Sweep Up Stairs Floors	Finish the Sweeping
	Mop Kitchen	Clean Bath Rooms
WEEK #2	Office-Up Stairs	Living Room Dusting
	Dust Up Stairs	Dining Room Dusting
	Sweep Outside Ft./Bk.	Silver Polish (2 or 3 items)
	Deck & Patio	Care China Cabinet (1 shelf)
WEEK #3	Sweep Downstairs	Ironing—(Do Catch up)
	Dust Downstairs	Sweep Books/Dust
	Myrna's Office	Arrangement of Books
	Bathrooms Clean	Storage (Projects need)
WEEK #4	Up Stairs Projects	Clean Kitchen Cabinets
	Air Vents/Light Fixture	Refrigerator Outside
	Clean Windows (2 Rm)	Stove (as needed)
WEEK #5	Straighten Storage	Clean Windows (3 Rms)
	Storage Room/Closets	Straighten Up Drawers
	Office (Filing/Other)	Stow Holiday Decorations
	Clean Down/Windows	Clean closet/seasonal
	Decorate for Holiday	Straighten Utility Storage

An added benefit of being totally responsible for yourself is you can dare to be you. And other secrets that have been carefully guarded can be dropped or dealt with.

Let's take this new freedom to the level of becoming our true destiny. We have liberty to go to an increased God consciousness level.

Now you may discretely (Some gossips will destroy you—so be guarded with whom you share the real you.) reveal and dismantle a hidden marriage or divorce, a child

34

you adopted out, a hidden abortion, any legal problem, your anorexic—DIET or an eating pattern, compulsive obsessive behavior problems, excessive EXERCISE. Defeat any secret holding you captive.

The goal I felt pulled to is to expose, face, deal with and become free of all prideful behaviors. At the same time becoming a more stable and wise adult. If you avoid responsibility—this will be a daring adventure! Yet, it will allow you to become your destiny.

This is repeated later, but make note of this important information.

NOTE

✓ You may receive up to $10,000 in free will money gifts without reporting them as income for any year.

✓ Insurance benefits on your mate are not taxable. They belong to the beneficiary, usually the mate, and are most helpful in dealing with the costs of a funeral. Operate in wisdom and take your time about any money decisions.

✓ Any gift check or cash made out to your name is yours and may be used to do any of the funeral costs or at your discretion.

✓ By the same token there is a maximum amount that can be given to children each year without taxes. Wise parents check this out for your state and take advantage of this provision.

CHAPTER EIGHT

DESIGN AND WORK YOUR PAPER PLAN

Again, relax! The funeral is over.

Oh, another paper just came in the mail? The companies love you. And they will keep sending you notices, etc. which will need to be handled, now or later! They wait. They will continue waiting until a man is sent to your door—that will happen if you wait too long! So decide to Schedule or not to Schedule. The best choice is to start with the task of managing your new life and leaving a good ending for your loved one.

What's Your Plan? It is strongly suggested you have one. Start forming it now. Get the spiral notebook we talked about before and start making some notes.

The areas to work on in PAPER WORK are:

- **Phone calls**, Flower, Thank You notes sent and Gift lists, etc.
- **Phone calls**: List 1. who called, 2. when, 3. any specific instructions or 4. greeting

The funeral home may have given you a booklet that has a place for the listing of names of ones who called—so no matter who answered the phone there could be knowledge of the caller's action.

If the calls are recorded, with an "I will arrive at the airport, please have someone meet me" message, then it can be known by the needed persons. Otherwise the cracks in the continuity get very large and people will fall into them. Maybe a very important person will, without this record.

- **Flowers, Gifts and Thank You notes** sent need to be carefully recorded. The tags from the flowers sometimes do not have last names. You may need help with that or with the addresses for the thank you notes.

The list of flowers and gifts such as food, money or services need to be accurate. Ask for help with this type of things.

Remember, your primary function at the funeral is to greet the people who have come to honor you and your mate.

Others will keep accurate lists of the floral arrangements, food gifts, and money gifts. Thank them for the assistance-it would be good to write a thank you note to them too. Maybe give a small gift to a strong helper. Some will be willing to address the envelopes of known entries.

- **NOTE:** You may receive up to $10,000 in free will money gifts without reporting them as income for any year. Any gift check or cash made out to your name is yours and may be used to do any of the funeral costs at your discretion. (By the same token there is a maximum amount that can be given to children each year without taxes. Wise parents take advantage of this provision.)

You will find that friends will help you and share generously at a time of loss like you are experiencing.

- **Receive graciously. It's easier to give and you'll have opportunities in the future. For now, receive thankfully.**

Give money gifts above costs to a favorite charity if that is what your mate would have wanted. It is wise to take your time so that you are certain all the expenses are taken care of—then share as you like.

Be certain to place postage and the correct return address on the thank you notes. It may save having to send another address notice in the future.

- **Food Gifts** often have an added dimension: there is a dish to be returned. If the food came from your church—return the dishes to the church and advise that the dishes from the wonderful food are in the church kitchen.

When neighbors or family are involved, well, you'll ask them to help you, or take them home and thank each person for their loving assistance. These are total blessings! The ones who do not have returnable dishes are the sweetest gifts—no need for a return! Please remember to thank all who provided food.

- **Collect the mail** and separate it into the notices of 1) **bills** to be paid and other 2) **correspondence** and 3) **magazines** and advertisement flyers.

Bills need to be handled in a timely way—so they must be in a primary position.

Your check book will need to be balanced and totally up to date so you do not have any problem. Remember, if you receive Social Security as a direct deposit—they will draft the account of your mate's current month of benefits. Expect it. The benefits for the month of April (this is for example—date of deposit varies) are deposited on the 25th day of March. So, if loved one deceased on 15th—you'll be back drafted for the whole month of April.

They do settle up later and deposit the token death benefit of $255.00 soon after you take the Death Certificate to their office. The funeral home usually notifies them before you have had time to do this.

Check the **correspondence** as you have time. Some may be sympathy cards, and some may have another gift in them. Now, you'll need to add that name to the gift list and get a thank you note out to them too. Make another list of the thank you notes you've sent. (Unfortunately, I sent two thank you notes to two couples. Ups!)

Notify other correspondents of your spouse's decease and whatever else is needed for that situation.

The **periodicals have an address usually it is inside** the front cover—or on a second or third page, with the change of name or address information you will need. **Clip the address label** from your magazine to return to them so they get the needed information for the changes you request. If you send a letter you can tape all the information to one sensible page and hopefully they change it.

- **Lists of Bequeathed items**
  In the spiral near the end of the listing of the business and insurance accounts there is a list of the items that were to be sent to my step daughter. They included items such as:

- **Items for Shug**: Packed, box in study closet, sent UPS 2nd day (Expensive!): Shipping number recorded and (date sent)
  Grandpa Etheridge's pocket watch in a case.
  Pop's glasses,
  Grandma Etheridge's eye glasses
  Bible given to Pop . . . dates such and such by Shug
  Favourite watch
  Pop's cap
  Pop's gift ring from Shug (The list was long and detailed)

Items for . . . as needed for your family
Items for Nephews:
Items for special ministry friends:
We used a name and items on each list. Then we recorded a copy of each list! Referrals to it answered questions because my memory was still stressed.

PAGES within the spiral notebook, These are listed without all my lengthy end results which were messy notes. Areas that proved complicated or difficult about which you may need to know what I learned are more detailed.

Priority positions of very important business items are first or close to it.

- The first was DuBail Judge. (They are my legal protection provider. Your lawyer will be your legal help source.) What I wanted to know or do were:
  - What was needed to get my will updated?
  - How to remove my Spouse's name from this legal service's membership?
  - Register my new address with them
  - What do I do with my spouses' will? What about Probate Court?

DuBail told me after three calls-(That's when I got to the person—the one I needed.) what to do in Missouri.

(Warning: each state has legal differences, SO, ASK!)

1. Do a new will (They sent the information form to be filled in and returned to them.) Next, when they sent the formal will, I had to have it witnessed (by two persons), certified and then made two copies. They advise keeping the original in a safe or secured location; and, I wanted the executor and my sister to each have a copy in their possession.
2. Called a lawyer in Cape to find out about the Probate Court in my area. (I found out the name of the secretary from the lawyer friend. Then I went to her at Probate.)
3. Go to Probate Court and it required that I go and take: The Will and Death Certificate to the County Probate This, for me, was a trip to the Division in Cape Girardeau at the Old Court House, in the office on Lorimar and answer the following questions:
   a. Present to Probate: the Will and Death Certificate (6/27/09 I presented them)
   b. Filed the will—with no assets (Telling them there are no assets—means no property is listed in only your spouses' name) [If you have property in only one name—add another name! Do not leave it that way. Do it ASAP!]
   c. State (SAY) to them: "Probate does not need to 'open this will'." (If both names are **not** on real property you will need to "open the will.")
   d. When you have no children to inherit your things—to keep assets out of probate you may:
      i. Do a Title on Death "TOD" or a
      ii. Beneficiary Deed to your assets
4. Collect a receipt for the recording of the will (They sent it back 7/9/09). File the receipt with your spouse's permanent records and a copy of the presented will. Yes, do a file.

This first one is VERY IMPORTANT! DO IT! (After the will was filed my auto title needed to be changed.) The TOD I placed on my recently **paid off** automobile title was written in when I changed the title ownership to me and my sister's names. So, at my death—no sweat! The auto will automatically be hers, **Title On Death**. (I do not desire more probate hearings after the fact if it can be easily avoided!) You will need the old title, and pay the small fee to do the Retitle with a TOD added. (You'll need the VIN number of the auto and the social security number of the TOD person for the paper work at the license bureau.) While you are doing this, check the date on your driver's license. You can get it renewed at the same place—if needed. Mine was about to run out—so I redid it too—same trip.

I couldn't do this with my real property, because it is **not debt free** as of this time. If I did the other option, **Beneficiary Deed**, she would have to PAY OFF the loan immediately upon my death. Not good for her! So, she'll have to deal with the property after I'm deceased.

As you work though all of these items **keep** the
1) Names of people who work with you
2) Phone numbers of key persons and the
3) Specific things you are to do **written down**

Written down because the stress level is so high, if/when you forget you can be easily reminded of the process thus far. (Notice: The probate took from death May 31 to filing June 7 to July 5, '09 to get the receipt back to me.)

- Record the names: of the company
- The people you talk with, Their phone number/s and any extension (X) for that person
- Find the customer service number on statements, credit cards or communication from the company you are working to update; and note if there is a best time to call a lawyer/company. (That's when you got the best service.)

Remember: one page for each service or company—use the right page of the spiral so you have the possible use of two pages for information you gather. For example Du Bail Judge has five phone numbers and three names. The lawyer and secretary were the only two names and two numbers. This was just to get to Probate Court to file the will, change an address and get a new will in progress.

Title Company to be contacted is the same one used when you purchased your property. Locate the Escrow # and date of purchase on the paper work from the purchase of your home.

Talk with the office manager. She tells me you need a lawyer to do the name change. (This item is yet to be finished.) Later there needs to be a change in Owner/s Name on the Title of my home.

Call the Bank holding the mortgage. They said it is not necessary to change the name on the title at this time. The loan department said the co-signer is responsible for the loan if one co-signer dies. It is best to wait until it is paid off.

Lawyer said it is not necessary at this time, but should be changed to include a second name.

Both mates' names were on the Title. Now only one living person's name is on it—mine.

My niece and/or sister could buy the home from my estate or they could sell it and divide the assets. NOTES: Best not to do a Beneficiary Deed because they would need to pay off any mortgage in full at that time. A TOD could be done when the home is paid in full.

Auto Title You already know about this from the entry above, but I have a page of notes. The loan company had to send a letter of release from the loan number, address of lender; before the Title could be re-titled in my name and the TOD information added. The new title is filed with the important papers as of July 8th. All these changes take time and effort. Remember, do the tasks one by one.

Insurance

Life: Old American Ins. (They held Dr. Grady's Policy.) Notify company of Dr. Grady's death. Send Death Certificate, Policy Number, Address change for Shug's coverage. Mix up in beneficiary got straightened out. Policy surrendered.

Life-Mass Mutual Myrna's Policy still in force; requested change of beneficiary form. Filled out form Policy No, etc. then returned to company. Premium: remains set to auto draft from personal checking account. In force until age 75. Evaluate need with my age at 70. (Plan for a pre-need burial to be bought—starting soon. Arrange to go to a seminar to learn about Pre-Need benefits. Attending this seminar was well worth the time invested.)

Accident AD&D This policy is accident death policy through the bank—most banks have them. It is auto drafted once each three months from the personal checking account. Usually the husband is the one with the policy in his name. Request it be changed to your name and do a Beneficiary change. If you have more than one checking account you will need to do the same for each one. Account, company and Policy No. dates, etc.

Auto Insurance Company, Policy No., coverage checked, Added underinsured motorist, others remained the same. Need to do name change, added another driver's name to coverage, address updated. Take your policy with you so you are prepared to fill out several forms at the office. It took a couple of billings to get it totally in order.

Home Owners Insurance Take the company name, policy number and information needed to do changes for beneficiary change. By the time of the six month renewal they had the name change and showed Grady's death. I added my executor as the new beneficiary, deleted spouse's name. That was so that I wouldn't have to change it again soon. Coverage added earthquake insurance, otherwise stayed the same.

Income Sources
Annuity Board Address, Contact, Phone for Customer service (from their news letter). Contact and change the name on the automatic deposit to the same personal checking account. Call someone like a local church secretary for help. She assisted me in getting the right phone numbers. Changed to widow's benefit from minister's benefit, supplied the information they requested. Then I asked: "What amount will be direct deposited, and on what day?" Have the Policy # when you call. Request had to be sent to them by mail. Do the letter and make a copy for "the file."

Social Security Take with you: both your social security numbers, date and place of births, marriage records—including former marriage dates, names, proof of service in the military (discharge papers), copy of your marriage certificate (They made copies of these.), record of earnings, copy of personal IRS for the previous year, copy of death certificate, also have the account number and information on the bank account that you want to receive the automatic deposit of your benefit. Ask what day the deposit can be expected. Wait until after the first deposit time then determine if the right account received the amount they told you to expect. Go by your bank, call or if you are on line www check the balance. DO NOT assume the amount is there without checking at least this first time. A death benefit of $255.00 should also arrive in the account. Your benefit should be the same as before for the month your spouse died. They will pay you the adjusted amount (the one they told you at their office) the next month. The deductions for Medicare and Part B, etc. for you will remain the same. The cost for your mate should not be deducted. If it is, go back and tell the customer service representative. You will be able to check the status of your file online in five days. I changed my password a month later.

Investments Name of agent, agency or company and stock certificate number, date of purchase. Inform customer service of the name change and add another, status change and address update. Unless you plan to dispose of the stock, nothing else needs to be done until such time as you decide to sell your holdings or transfer the ownership.

Bank Accounts Go to the customer service representative of the bank with the account to have your spouse's name removed and add another. You will need a Death Certificate and the person/s with you to add them to the account. Change your address at this time, but you will probably need to verify the address change by mail. You can continue to use the checks with the old information—writing in the new, but there will come a time you need to reorder and update the information. Remember to take all the social security numbers of persons being added to the accounts.

All bank accounts will need to be changed:
Checking
Savings
Loans

Yearly Registrations for Not-for-Profit Organizations
File such forms in a timely way or the corporation ends.

Sole Proprietor companies accounts may need to be updated—depending upon the proprietor—If that was your mate's you can let the company end the year of their death or make changes in city, state and federal Numbers for the company. You must make that decision before January 1 the next year!

Telephones Cable Satellite Radio and all other binding contracts will need to be honored as per their terms—or you could have cancellation fees. Check the paper work to find out the dates and agreements. Telephones need to be changed to your name as quickly as possible. Your social security number will have to be added to most phone accounts to change the name. Call the customer service number on the phone bill and keep calling until you get what you need completed.

Credit Cards Get out the stack of them and write the card name, customer service number, card number and the date of expiration. The Fuel credit cards were the most difficult ones to get changed, but American Express was the ultimate! I wrote letters to each company requesting the card in my name—two were already in my name—with the address change. Several cancelled the cards—their choice. I called before and after the letter requesting the change in address and name. The letter is standard for them.

Gasoline companies
Department Stores
Visa
Master charge
Discover
American Express

WARNING FOR WIDOWS: If you do not have at least one credit card in your name before your husband dies you will probably experience problems. The credit card companies find that widows and divorced women consistently have had the most difficulties with paying their bills. Get a card with your name on the card—before this time—if possible.

Hospital and Medical Primary Care Bills will continue to come in for several months. Keep a file and try to remember the dates of appointments, the doctors who visited in the hospital and the other costs such as the prescriptions. Write them down—compare the bills and make sure you pay only the bills. Medicare will notify you, and then later—sometimes months later, will tell you what you owe of the bill. Pay only the amount and ones you owe.

Internet Services or Connections Email addresses, Face Book, other memberships having to do with www? You will need to send a **broadcast email** or Face Book comment regarding your spouse's death. You can close the accounts, or not—that is your choice. I sent out over 200 notices about Dr. Grady's death because of the ministry contacts.

- Work Details and Planning for Accounts
- Take some time each week, but the first few weeks do lots of calls and trips to the banks, Social Security, etc., etc., etc.!

- You must keep notes, then, later record the passwords, etc. Into a permanent notebook for just that type of information. Then KEEP it secure. The ones you had or learned existed or set up need to be written.
- Keep encouraged, and try to laugh. The people trying to help you are only following their company's orders.
- Don't stop until you're finished with a project. Some may take lots of time—even daily work for a week.
- Remember the email addresses, passwords, etc.? Try to find your mate's list—usually they are written.
- Details of Accounts The notes you make will be a vital help in the months to come. I've located two items that I need to continue working on during this writing. Also, finally I've remembered where I put all the originals of birth certificates, etc. (My executor will be happy about that.)
- Other Items and what to do with them:
  - Passport cancellation of an active passport: Letter to CLASP requesting they cancel the active Passport of Dr. Grady (See sample letter at end of this chapter.)
  - Driver's Licence keep secure
  - Union Cards keep secure
  - Ordination Agencies keep secure
  - Alma Mata notification and transcripts, keep secure
  - Special Technology-hearing aid Learned just last month that the hi-tech hearing aids could be recycled by a company associated with the (sales company's) people who were so very patient with Dr. Grady's often stopped up hearing aids. I gifted his to them so another person could have some help as a gift.
  - Head Stone-order, install and check on place-ment was done by Shug. She needed copies of Death Certificate, Military papers, etc. They'll tell you what. The funeral home really doesn't want to deal with these military head stones. They do not make a profit on them. The Veterans' organizations will help you with aged warriors and with the active duty losses the military is great! Placement of the marker is an expense.
  - Deed to Garden of Peace for four Lots, I sent the Etheridge family plot deed to Shug. I decided to place Dr. Grady in Lot 1, beside Marie, His first wife in Lot 2 leaving 3 and 4 for Shug's use.

- Settle up with family members For example: husband's daughter. If you go beyond the call of duty there are far fewer to no complaints.
- Remind family members of items such as: I don't have your mother and dad's marriage license

The following list and notes were recorded in my **spiral notebook that I starting after the funeral** as I changed an address, called, changed names on other items.

The first page is

Always, **keep notes** of what you have done—be warned you will forget something or other. **The notes are your security net**. Do them religiously! Be **accurate and consistent** in what you do for each entry.

PAPER WORK

Paper Work Details are worth the work, because of the peace you will have knowing your business things are in proper order.

Active Passport Cancellation Request:
(Please return cancelled passport to My . . . (your name), his widow)
Name and Your Inside Address City, State Zip

Date of letter

TO: ATT: Dorothy
Fax: 202-955-0256
Consular Lost and Stolen Passports
ATT: CLASP
1111 19th ST. NW, Suite 500
Washington, DC 20036

ATT: CLASP Representative,

This letter is to inform you that I, Myrna (Your Name), widow of Name (of your partner) request that the passport for my deceased husband (wife), Name as it is on Passport, issued (date of issue) November 25, 2008 be cancelled and returned to me at the above address. Enclosed please find a copy of his death certificate and his passport.

If you have any question, please contact me directly at (area code) Number where they will talk with you.

Thank you for your help in safe-guarding this important and returning this sentimental document to me.
Sincerely,
(My name)
RE: Passport Number: 1234567
Name on Passport Grady . . . .
Born (Month, day, year) Deceased (Month, day year.)
(Later I sent a thank you to the lady, Dorothy, who helped with this.)

> *When the paper work is back to*
> *Your normal, it is amazing how long the day seems.*
> *Your second job is completed.*
>
> *M. Etheridge's Widowhood Thoughts*

Remember this truth as you go through one of the most difficult days of your life.

> *I can do all things through Christ,*
>
> *(THIS TRUTH GIVES ME ENERGY FOR TODAY)*
> *which strengtheneth me.*
>
> *Philippians 4:13 AMP*

50

The Do You Know Where It Is List
  Your Will
  Passport
    US Dept. Health Inoculation
  Title to you auto/s
  Title to your property
  Insurance Policies
    Life
    Property
    Auto
    Accident
    Drug Coverage
    Medicare
  Birth Certificate
  Marriage License
  Durable Power of Attorney
  Tax Receipts
    Property
    Personal Property
    Income IRS, State
Royalty Information

Dr. Myrna truly cares about what you are facing.

For ministry, conferences, books or prayers contact:
© Myrna L. Etheridge, Etheridge Publishing
2128 William #164
Cape Girardeau, Missouri 63703-5847
For Telephone numbers and email visit:
www.gmeministries.org
www.CysticFibrosisSupportOrg.org

CHAPTER NINE

THE FINANCE FACTOR

Living within your Means, Money, Planning and Dumb Decisions (now costing you) are all part of your financial situation.

My husband was extremely wise in church affairs and guidance for others. But, how was he about our own finances? Well, the following will indicate an area of personal weakness.

We had attended an enlightening and challenging teaching on fasting. I overheard my husband say to a colleague: "There are four main hungers of man: for food, for water, for knowledge and for power. I've decided to give up knowledge for four days." (Actual quote, Dr. Grady Etheridge, 1984)

The colleague was astounded—maybe horrified. Everyone laughed except yours truly, his wife and the colleague. As they laughed and I smiled, I thought,

> *"And think (now as a widow) he was the one to whom I listen*
> *and show respect?*
> *No wonder our finances*
> *Are always a challenge!"*
>
> *M. Etheridge's widowhood thoughts*

On the way home there was my decision to fast for four days—on water or diluted juice! My need was for a securely correct data source.

Facing Weakness

Maybe your mate had a weakness that affected you and everything about your relationship? Only the wisdom of the creator can be an ultimate source. Counselors are a help, but the decision is still ours.

Stop the Angers. You can. It is your decision, just do it.

Once the funeral was over and the joy of the love my friends showed in supplying the need for the funeral expenses was less vivid in my mind, I had to deal with the anger. Within me there was strong anger for the stupid things I gave O.K. to and for which I was equally responsible along with my husband. Now I was bearing the end results.

Friends in Canada, Pastor Smith's family, sent me a ticket to come to the beautiful Maritimes area for ministry and a rest time. They patiently listened to my comments and reassured me that God had been faithful to supply what was needed at the time it was needed. (In retrospect, my anger was showing. It was ugly, but they loved me/us!)

After all, the total amount of the cost of the funeral, grave opening and head stone were provided! I didn't have a debt from that, though there were still hospital and doctor bills to be satisfied. Even the hospital bill was later paid in full! Somehow, each time a doctor's bill arrived, I had the money to pay it. Truly, as my friends were pointing out—God is faithful! (He will be for you too, if you serve and live for Him.)

My anger at the limited resources of the thirty years of my married life was a fire in my mind.

As a middle thirties woman my income was comfortable—even more than I needed. Now as a seventy plus senior, it was not comfortable! I was angry!

The truth was: My need was for forgiveness more than for finances.

When I realized that my 'sod hut in Oklahoma man's life' was very good as he saw it from his reference point. I had expected MUCH more than the joy of a sod hut dug into the soil of the Red River valley!

The forgiveness came with a flood of tears. They flowed over the banister of the deck looking to the eastern sky and the Atlantic Ocean. God even sent a full rainbow—the book cover—just to reassure me. He is my source, my husbandman. Though difficult for me now, Grady did what he felt was good. Even when he bought a second auto and I boo hoed for two days. (We had just paid off the loan on the one he traded in. I was away ministering to hopefully meet our other obligations with the offerings.) He didn't see it that way. I was heartbroken and exhausted. My tears cleared the memory of the looming financial disaster.

My friends loved me and Dr. Grady, and gently helped me to see the need for forgiving him for doing what seemed O.K. to him. They assured me God would help me since I'd remained faithful to my call to ministry and peacefully served my husband.

Credit Card problems

When my time of rest was over I went to the annual conference of my ordaining ministry covering, International Ministers' Forum, in Dayton, Ohio. The condolences continued and many lamented, or celebrated Grady's life and journey to Heaven. I cried some, but was gaining strength.

The downside was the hotel had to be on the credit card. And on the way home the transmission on our/my auto began showing signs of failure. That's when the credit card problems started. I'll told you about changing the names and address on them in the Paper Changes.

Never put more on the credit card than you can pay off in a month unless it is a major item. You must need it to function so it will be worth the interest it will cost for an extended pay off.

The stress of a constantly living beyond your means is too wearying. Do not do it. Change your spending habits. Avail yourself of a resale shop. Wear the same suit with a new shirt and tie. Change your diet, whatever, but, live within your means.

Some will need to find a less expensive place to live. Do not sell your home as a senior until there is no other recourse. Try to remain where you are for at least two years so your emotions can recover and you can feel comfortable. The sale of a home can be expensive, exhausting, and time consuming. Besides moving is the pits as well as costly! After 39 relocations, believe me—I know this! Most seniors do not have sufficient income to negotiate another home loan. This could be your last home if you do not have ample resources or securities.

To go into a rental you will need two months of rent and a deposit to make the deal. Moving itself is costly in money and energy! Avoid making many changes. It is very stressful for new singles. Besides apartment living is usually too many people and more noise than you want.

The Widower reflects:

Why was she so angry? The food was on the table
Why shouldn't I eat. She's so slow
And what do we need a serving spoon for any way?
(Must have been a woman thing.)

M. Etheridge's Widowhood Thoughts

Widowhood is
Making choices to change expenses
So you will be able to live
Within your means.
That's far less stressful than
Facing the facts of debt.

M. Etheridge's Widowhood Thoughts

CHAPTER TEN

YOUR PHYSICAL: BODY, FOOD, EXERCISE, CLOTHES, AND FACTORS

Body

The body! Oh, the body! The hair will usually start falling out four to six months into the loss time. Other changes can follow—if you forget to live wisely.

Joanie, my trusted friend and "beautician magnifico" shared this fact with me. She commented when I was in for the 5th week regular color and cut, "You haven't lost as much hair as most widows do."

My view was, I was concerned because I was losing enough extra hair that I asked her, "Is this the usual thing for widows?"

Her years of experience spoke up accurately, exact, "Well, for the widows who've been my clients—it is very usual. You're doing very well, but then you eat healthy. Most usually—well, they do not eat wisely. Mourning and loss almost always affects hair growth, but sometimes they start having various other health problems."

"Guess I'd better watch out?" I asked.

"Yes, rest, diet and emotions really affect our bodies. It shows in the hair first—I think." Joanie added, "Look at all this new hair growth!"

Food

I saw the new hair and it was encouraging! Having taught Biology and having studied Home Economics, vitamins, food, rest and exercise were part of my life; these were not new subjects for me. The first year there were my changes in vitamins. And there were other efforts to make my physical gain back strength that had been taken away by the stresses of loss.

Some other problem areas are joints, arthritis or other infections due to the stresses coupled with poor diet and aging in general. After all the years are adding weaknesses for some of us anyway.

Upon thinking back to that conversation my change was that my vitamin regiment had been doubled; and, I forced myself to eat living fruit and veggies at least once a day while drinking lots of really good filtered water. Why? Because I'd noticed that my hair was becoming dry and fragile and falling out more than usual. You may want to check your hair and finger nails too.

This action was taken about two months into my loss. Maybe earlier would have been wiser—but the changes have reversed considerably by the time of this writing. Yes, there is repair!

When I'm traveling and ministering (working) more than three times a week or writing four to six hours per day, vitamins are usually increased to compensate for the added stress.

"What vitamins," you ask?

Many sources provide reliable supplements that can help you. Choose your own or call me at the number in this book, and as a distributor for a very outstanding company we can explore your need and point to some possible workable solutions. A local health food store will help, if you ask. Sensible eating, rest and exercise bring a balance back to your body.

Exercise
Continual good health depends upon the support of good food, rest and sensible exercise. Do not start lifting 240 pounds of weights when you've never done 50 pounds! Be sensible! I'd love to be the woman champion for a 200 pound press, but I need to do 30 or 50 and work my way up! So I decided to start with a pedometer. (You can smile or laugh, but that's what I did.)

Get a pedometer—they are reasonably priced. Find out how many steps you are taking in your average day. What I learned was that in most days my total steps

58

were over 5,000. That's almost a mile. During a regular day inside the house that's what I walk with a flight of steps between upstairs and my work area down stairs.

Some days the pedometer recorded 9,600 steps. It varies and probably will for you too.

If your knees complain check out the possibility of aquatic exercise classes. Usually there is a center near you. The key is: Do it! Exercise the best way for your body and work up a sweat if possible.

Sometimes it can be a joy to work. My yard had lots of leaves this year and the city faithfully comes by and vacuums (I call it slurping my leaves.) them after I gather them to a huge raked windrow in the front yard. My goal was five wheelbarrow loads a day until the leaves were gathered from the back and front yard to the proper place. During the eight days outside I sang, enjoyed the work, burned calories and toned up my muscles. Sure enough the city "slurped" my leaves. And I was so pleased with myself that I splurged with ice cream on a piece of pie at the family Thanksgiving dinner.

You saw the chart for house cleaning in Chapter Seven—it works and is a great way to exercise and enjoy the results.

Many of us will not have ample funds to hire a house cleaning service, so this plan is ideal. In six hours a week you will achieve a pleasant, orderly, clean, well maintained home. We'll not mention the exercise!

Within a year all the tasks needing to be done to maintain a home will be done each month. Once a year all the tasks—even odd ones are completed once and some are done three times in a year. My experience is that my five week schedule works, if you work it. You can start any month and any week of a month, do what's to be done for that week and get great results. My refrigerator has it posted, so it is handy. Miss a day? Oh, catch up!

Clothes
Laundry is another thing, but if you are single you can begin doing your laundry every two weeks. All you need do is supply yourself with undies and linens for two weeks.

Get brave and look in your closet or wherever you keep your clothing. Answer some questions, please:

Do you wear the clothes in there?

How often?

Which ones were your departed's favorites?

Do you like those favorites?

Now, let's do something. Let's separate your clothing.

1) **Things I like and wear.** Place them **front and center** of the closet.
2) Things **I like that are worn out. Clean** them and **discard** them. Get a plastic bag for the clean ones and mark it "Yellow House" or whatever recycling agency is near you.
3) Wrong size? Fat and Skinny clothes need to become a thing of the past.
   a. Overweight? Eat smaller proportions and drink plenty of WATER!
      i. Keep only next size down
      ii. Get the other wrong sizes out of your closet! Give them to someone (Be certain they will not be offended.) or some agency. YEAH! Your closet grew.
   b. Too Thin? Eat regular meals. Cut back to one—SOLO—cup of coffee! Drink more water and eat when you are hungry. One size up-only-get the rest out of the closet.
4) Shopping—RED FLAG WARNING—beware if you are compulsive about shopping keep the following warnings.
   a. Know what you NEED
   b. Know you can afford an item before you go shopping for it
   c. See other things in your closet and determine how any new item can be mixed and matched
   d. Never buy an item you do not NEED or that does not fit you right now!

Clothes shopping can be a trap and increase the stress of limited finances. Money limits can make your mind feel like shutting down.

Do not allow yourself to buy clothing on credit cards. Remember it is best to pay off any credit card each month. If you cannot do this—don't buy anything you can do without. No, nothing! Content yourself. Go look in your closet, the storage closet and the walk-in closet. See how you are blessed. Contentment with Godliness is great gain.

If you never handled the finances of your family you may need to get help. When the funds you have are well managed usually there is sufficient money for your needs. Some wants may need to wait, but usually the needs are handled.

Some of you—like my experience—do not have a sufficient supply. If we would be better off with more, we need to explore finding some income source to sustain us. That's O. K. and do not panic. You will find what you need. Keep on looking for the right work for you.

Life will not be very enjoyable if you continue to feel stressed financially. Plan out what needs to be done. Ask trusted friends or professional advisors to help you get past this trying time. Consider selling items of value that are not important to you, but do not give them away by selling them for less than they are worth.

> *Widowhood is*
> *Facing the checkbook and praying to God*
> *For guidance or an outright miracle*
> *To pay your necessary bills.*
>
> *M. Etheridge's Widowhood Thoughts*

Other
Reading is a resourceful way to go on a vacation with very little expense or energy investment.

A favorite wholesome or funny movie is a rest to your mind. Take vacations from the day to day tasks. Even a meal out with the guys or girls can change you mental attitude. Yes, the loss is difficult, but bake cookies and watch a movie to pamper yourself!

You are worth every effort! Try to find reasons to laugh—belly laugh as often as you can. It changes the mental atmosphere about you instantly. Once a doctor laughed his way out of a serious illness with Laurel and Hardy! Even something so small as the battle between the local squirrel and the red bird can cause a laugh! DO IT! DO IT OFTEN! Get a library card and a book of jokes.

Study
If you've wanted to get computer literate—take a class offered by the local college or business school. Buy a book and read it before you try to work with the new soft ware program.

Learn a new language or develop your hobby into a fund raiser source.

Spend time perfecting your artistic abilities or musical skills.

Writing
Consider putting your experiences of life down for the next generation. There's nothing like a firsthand account of the history of your family.

No, you do not need to do all this at once. Spend thinking time and then put some creative action with your thoughts. Meanwhile, do the paper work.

Relationships
There has been very little mention of developing a new relationship with the opposite sex.

The reason is: you need to have time for healing and closure toward your departed mate. Value the years—even if he/she spent you into a bad place. Settle the joys and hurts and come to a place of enjoying life so you'll be pleasant company.

Your physical may scream, but for many of us who have had a mate who was ill for some time—you need to ignore your physical need. That's not to say it is not real, but it is not necessary to go there at this time. A quick fix can be disastrous! It is best to adjust to being alone.

For the last week of my husband's life we had lots of hugs and kisses to remember. They sustain me even now. He'd get a drink of water and a kiss and hug. There are no regrets, but tears do come to my eyes when I think of that time. When I can think of that week and not tear up—I'll know I'm emotionally healed. (I'm not there yet. Are you?)

Wait for the perfect time and the perfect relationship. It is worth the wait. Some second rate choice could devastate years of your life. II Corinthians 7 says, 'that if you are without wife—don't seek one. If you have one—don't seek freedom.' Paraphrase Myrna. Also there are other truths in that chapter you may want to review sometime this first year.

Please, remember it is wisdom to follow a "no decision for two years" guideline. Our emotions need to heal so we can make quality decisions.

Where will I live? Shall I own? Rent? Sell? Stay here?

Seniors may be faced with the possibility of not being able to qualify for another home loan so if they decide to sell their home—they can't relocate and own their home. They would need to pay the entire amount of the home or have sufficient securities to back their loan before they could buy again.

Selling a home can take a long time, and there may be other financial expenses of repairs to the home before it is marketable.

Seek able advisors and take your time. Even the relocation costs of rental can be several thousands of dollars. Rent, advance and deposit soon mount up to a considerable sum. You will need to decide and work a plan.

Changes are very stressful and particularly so for the newly single widow or widower. Mental stress causes reactions not responses. These knee-jerk reactions can be very damaging.

Remember a rule of thumb is: it is best to refrain from major decisions for two years.

Advisors and Planning Help
These persons are available and you may want to seek out friends or others who are skilled advisors. Remember to think deeply and take your time.

There is safety in multiple advisors and prayer! I found myself praying for guidance to be given by ones who didn't know about what was happening to me. The results were very helpful!

Think on this!

in the morning,
Gazing at the beauty of a sunrise,
While giving thanks for
Another day.
I'm aware
Though I'm not sharing it
With my human mate
I know that on the other
Side my Jesus is Rising early
Enjoying it with me.
Jesus' Spirit is comforting me.
Only Jesus Christ could do that!

M. Etheridge's Widowhood Thoughts

CHAPTER ELEVEN

SETTLE YOUR REST FACTORS

The Need to Do List for Wise Living includes:

A. Will for you

1. Redo the will (have a lawyer do it) and update it
2. Notarize it so it is legally binding
3. Needs to be properly completed and copies placed with key persons, Keep your original copy in a safe place (bank/safe)

B. Durable power of attorney is a two page (usually one sheet) document. Have it notarized and placed in an accessible place for quick use. My copy of this document is in my bill fold, another is in my personal business file with other Legal Documents. Its full title is Advance Directive for Healthcare Living Will/Durable Power of Attorney. The hospital can help you with this, as well as your lawyer so what you want done is carried out in case of illness or accident. (Visit Care Pages on the web for resources <news@newsletters.carepages.com.)

C. Deeds for your property (Changes? Recorded? Check about Beneficiary Deed if your property is paid off.)

D. License & Title to Auto/s (change names, get new title with name changes and use the TOD if the auto/s are paid for)

E. Income Taxes (copies of filed IRS Federal and State so they are easily found and current. Your spouse's last year of life allows for a joint return and the deduction for them for the whole year, even if they lived only a day.)

F.   Personal Property (autos, etc.) receipts for city/state taxes

G.   Real (land) Property Tax receipts and copies for city/state and state license plates

H.   Life Insurance policy and remember to pay your premiums. (Any insurance benefit paid to you is tax free. Your policy/s need to be with your personal papers.)

I.   Pre-Need Burial Decisions. Record them and file a copy with this collection of information. The funeral home will also keep a file of your requests for the Pre-Need memorial service and desires. Keep copies of payments or your Arrangement.

J.   Burial Plot. Determine where you will be placed. If you do not own the plot you will need to:

K.   Get Permission from the Key Person/s—Now! See the letter asking for approval letter. It's at the end of this chapter.

L.   Letters to request permission for burial rights/for plot use of the Cemetery. The original needs to be notarized and sent to the Cemetery. (Find Cemetery name, address and person to be sent to along with who and where information. You will want a copy with your information.) Again, see the end of this chapter for sample letters.

M.   Saving and checking account bank names and number of the accounts. All names of lawyer, accountant, insurance agent/s, and other financial representatives should be listed along with their contact information.

N.   List your basic information if you do not have a Pre-Need plan. Full name, maiden name, date of birth and social security number.

O. List all financial assets, liabilities and account numbers. Identify all bank accounts, safe deposit box information, insurance policies, and company benefits along with identifying numbers.

P. List all liabilities, such as mortgages, loans and credit card debt.

Q. Advise your will executor where all these documents are kept. List where your will, trust documents, tax returns and insurance policies are kept. Do regular updates so the information is accurate.

R. List of credit cards, Numbers, Customer Service phone, Digit from back, and any pins you've added, such as on debit checking account cards. Place in same safe place as the other documents.

S. Location of Passport—Does it need to be renewed? Make a copy of the information page so you have the number and all the other needed information in case it gets stolen or lost. Keep health list.

These will be accomplished more easily than you think. When you start organizing now, the rest is easy for you handle each item as it arrives.

Following are: Sample Letters: Regarding Burial Plot

The Request to Give Permission Letter is the first sample. This type cover letter is sent to the person who will be able to give you permission for burial in the plot or circumstance you are requesting.

Following is a letter to my person who could give permission. Hopefully, this will solve your need. The purpose of this letter is to get permission with as little effort on the part of the person being asked as possible. The need was for the official signature and a notary's verification. This letter officially determines where I want to finally rest. Yours could do the same.

This letter to request permission I desired was personally, one of the most difficult letters for me to compose, send and receive the response. The favor of my X was extended and I was very thankful!

The Helper is available.

Right now I remember that Widowhood is
Watching alone, crying part in remembrance
And part in sympathy
With Josephine
When Beth is well,—you know—in "Little Women"
But still no one hands me a hankie.
Yet, I'm not really
Alone because Jesus' Spirit is within me—comforting me.
Only Jesus Christ could do that!

M. Etheridge's Widowhood Thoughts

Notes:

Permission Letter Sample:

Your inside address with your
real telephone number needs to be here—
maybe email.

Name and Inside Address   **Date: of your letter**
Of person who is able
To grant you permission for burial
In a lot you do not own.

Dear (Person's Name),

May 2011 be a year of blessings and good times for your family. The (ministry and writing) continue to keep me occupied!

This has been a long time in coming, but I need a further favor. The (Cemetery plot's title) requires your written permission for my remains to be placed with the boys. Thank you for this bit of pain, but it will be very much appreciated.

The letter with information needed is enclosed. (I've enclosed 2 copies in case an extra is needed.)

The (Cemetery) Garden of Memories didn't have your current address or phone number on file either.

If you prefer to mail a copy straight to them, of if you want me to mail the original to them—either will be O.K. Probably it would be best if both you and I had a copy of the notarized document. I've enclosed a self addressed stamped envelope for your convenience. Do as seems best to you. I do want a copy, please.

Thank you for this help. I'm trying to leave everything in order since I've been out of the country so often.

Sincerely,

Your Signature and Name
(End of request to person letter)

(Send this letter with the request letter, to make the response easy.)
Form for Notary & Cemetery follows. (Date is at bottom.)
Name (of Permission Giver)
(Their Inside Address)

ATT: TO WHOM IT MAY CONCERN
Re: Permission to inter (your name) remains in son's plot at decease in (family name) plot with (Names of person/s) her (relationship to you) in the plot #___, Lot #___ in (Garden of Memories—use your cemetery name), located at city, state.
  c/o S. Memorial (cemetery owner address) and Phone: ( )-____—____
City State, Zip

ATT: (Your cemetery's Manager's Name,), Office Manager

Dear (Manager):

Thank you for receiving this notarized copy of my permission for (my name) (my address) (my phone) to place her remains in the same Lot where my (relationship to letter writer) are interred when the need arises.

I, (Name of Permission Giver), as the responsible person for the family Plot of four (be specific about this for your need) burial lots give permissions for this action in Lot #____when it is needed.

(Name of Permission Grantor)   **Date:**
Address of Grantor
Phone number of Grantor

I have witnessed this signature and affirm it:

Certified Notary-Term Expires: **Date:**
(End of Certified letter granting permission for burial.)

Yes, call for your need—
The Helper is available.

70

CHAPTER TWELVE

RE-ROOT
WHERE YOU ARE PLANTED

July found me relaxing on the back patio. The wind swayed the branches and the local bird population chirped away around the bird feeder on my tree. But for missing my partner who loved the deck glider as much as I do—I was content.

There were things still waiting for my decision, or some more paper work, but deep within me I knew that treasuring my time and being able to stay where we have lived for five years was a stabilizing decision. Many had asked me if I were going to move. My usual answer was, "For two years, I'm not deciding to do anything that makes a major change in the way I do life."

The "Oh—" drawn out to the full extent of an "oooo . . ." was a usual response. They usually took it like a put down, but I meant it as self-defense and stability. Besides, I didn't trust my judgment. The tears could pop out at any moment. And I knew it. I may have looked O.K., but that was not what was happening inside me.

The neighbors continued to be the kind I wanted and the neighborhood was one of the most convenient to all needed services that I had ever had the pleasure of living in. Why would I want or need to move?

My decision was to re-root right here where I am planted.

Even after the trip to Canada that decision seemed the best that could be made. The area was lovely. I've even chosen to use it as the cover for this book. It was a sight of loveliness into everything and nothing. Straight below the edge of the deck—beneath the rainbow, is a 230 foot drop off—the same type feeling as when you are left alone by the death of your mate.

My mental attitude was NO MORE CHANGES. I've had it with changes. First the funeral changed everything. Then the abundant postal mail needed to be sent to an address at a public area box, to make my home a bit more secure.

Finally, to save the cost of email service and free up the money for a web site server, the email service needed to be changed. That was a terrible change routine. There were over 600 email addresses to be retyped into the new account—a free one. The changes were very painful—very wearing on me. My patience, that was usually remarkable, was growing short!

During the 'first time' to see people they continued to learn of Grady's passing. Even during the fall Praise-A-Thon some of the participants were astounded that he had died three months earlier. That wasn't easy for me either. Yet, I was glad he was so loved—by more people than me. For that I rejoiced.

When the colors of autumn turned the trees into items of rare beauty, I was getting the address changes under control and only a few each week continued to drag in from the other mail sources. (We had three addresses at the time Grady left.) The end was nearly in sight. The files with all the things to be changed (that were crucial) had been taken care of. I even placed the files into a metal box and stowed it in the closet—not on the desk as during the first months.

Facing my humanity and vulnerability smacked me across the face. Will I, you, we, respond or react?

That, my friend, is your personal decision!

Forget about blaming anyone or anything else. I implore you choose for life and begin growing again. Life is for the living. Just as my mother said to me from the time I was a little girl. The years have proved what she taught me was correct. Life is for the living!

CHAPTER THIRTEEN

SETTLE YOUR DESTINATION

Look at me! I'm Living Eternity Bound! Do you have assurance as to where you would be if you were to die—right now? If not, let me assure you, you can know. Following this short snippet of what living with children close to death can involve, I will explain.

Kirk's, my first born son, was in the hospital—the orderlies and nuns were visiting him as a teaching case for cystic fibrosis. His lungs and heart were very compromised by all the infections. For being three and one half years old, a child in age, he was an emotional and intellectual giant.

He awoke and looked at all the people in white. The usual oxygen treatment was inside a mist tent, so he lifted the tent and asked matter-of-factly, "If I'm dead and in Heaven, where are Keif (He couldn't say Keith.) and Grandpa?" One of the nuns was totally shocked by the insight about the short distance from earth to Heaven that he understood as such a young child. She kindly reassured him, "Kirk, you are not dead and in Heaven. We are just checking on how well you are doing today. Please, rest."

He lay down. The brief exchange took place just a few days before he crossed over to Heaven—at three and a half years of age. Many weeks later this account was relayed to me by one of my friends from this excellent hospital in Jonesboro, Arkansas. Like you, I laughed and cried.

My young son knew where he was going and some who would be there waiting. Do you know this?

You can know for certain. The Book of St. John is a book written to tell you "You are loved." (If you are not certain where John's book is, look to the right side of the family Bible just past the start of the New Testament.) In fact, God loved the entire world.

He loved the entire world so much that He sent His only son to die in our place, so we could choose to serve Him and live with Him forever. If you have never read that book out loud as though it is written just to you—you will be blessed if you do. That's where my son's confidence came from and where mine comes from. Jesus Christ is my LORD and Savior.

The balancing of life is one important key to regaining your sense of self and self-worth. Dr. Grady for eight years worked with pastors in his denominational work. One gathering that was very special included an outstanding educator pianist who came from another state to play the famous and difficult Rachmaninoff Concerto and to share with the pastors.

All in all Dr. Grady was ill at ease with such brass. On the way from the St. Louis Air Port the Godly, College President was sharing that his mother and father had twelve other children. After the final boy was born his pastor father named him Theophilus. When a friend commented, "Oh, you must have loved Luke's gospel to name him that." the forthright, pastor drew in a breath. Then he honestly and wisely replied, "That was the-awfulest-look'n kid I even saw!" "That's why I named him that!"

They laughed, sort of embarrassed for the child. They were both thinking, dear little son, thirteenth child, now had a difficult name to overcome too.

The tenseness left Grady. The two, both remarkable men in their own rights, continued laughing. Finally, the wise collegiate leader added, "You can be serious about the LORD and His Word, but never get too serious about yourself, Brother Etheridge."

After all you've been through in this loss time remember it is best to find reasons to laugh at yourself—and at life in general. Being too serious can cause you to lose your joy. That is not a good thing because; joy provides a strength and hope for life to grow on and within.

74

God is watching over you, if you belong to Him.

Psalm 33:18 through 22 tells us *" . . . the LORD's eye is upon those who fear Him [who revere and worship Him with awe], who wait for Him and hope in His mercy and loving kindness, to deliver them from death and keep them alive in famine.*

Our inner selves wait [earnestly] for the Lord; He is our help and our shield. For in Him does our heart rejoice, because we have trusted (relied on and been confident) in His holy name.

Let Your mercy and loving-kindness, O Lord, be upon us, in proportion to our waiting and hoping for You."

We want to walk close to the Lord to retain our strength. Psalm 31:9-10 Amplified Bible verses give a vivid picture of what can happen if we get out of fellowship with our creator. *"Have mercy and be gracious unto me, O Lord, for I am in trouble; with grief my eye is weakened, also my inner self and my body. For my life is spent with sorrow and my years with sighing; my strength has failed because of my iniquity, and even my bones have wasted away."*

Iniquity is stubbornly continuing to do wrong when the wrong is known. That is a really unwise choice.

Personally *I would rather choose to be dwelling in the house of the Lord [in His presence] all the days of my life. Then we can expect that in the day of trouble He will hide us in His shelter; in the secret place of His tent will He hide us. He will set us high upon a rock.* Paraphrase Psalm 27:4-5.AMP

My Prayer for You:

May the peace of Jesus Christ's love comfort your being. Thank you, Father God, for walking this reader through the darkness and despair of the night of their loss. Without coming to You the new day that they are walking into would not be as bright or filled with sufficient hope for another stage of life.

May the presence of Your peace, Jesus, and Your Holy Spirit fill us with hope for the future. Amen.

Sincerely, I pray He is your strength and your stronghold of salvation.

He will help you if you ask. Just talk with Him the way you would with me. He's as close as your call to Him.

Jesus Christ of Nazareth can do something I could never do. He can live inside you and make you aware of His presence. Psalm 27:4 tells you why thinking on His help can truly change the way you see what has happened.

The results are eternally effective. This happens when you decide to turn to His ways and serve Him along with believing that He truly is the ultimate Prophet who did mighty miracles and is the eternal firstborn Son of the Most High God, the LORD God Jehovah.

For in the day of trouble He will hide me in His shelter;
In the secret place of His tent will He hide me;
He will set me high upon a rock."
Psalm 27:5 AMP

Jesus Christ is the true
Widow and Widower's Helper. Meet with Him today!

76

Dr. Myrna Etheridge ©photo 2011, Mississippi River, Cape Girardeau, Missouri

*   *   *

For ministry, conferences, books or prayers contact:
© Myrna L. Etheridge, Etheridge Publishing
2128 William #164
Cape Girardeau, Missouri 63703-5847
For Telephone numbers and email visit:
www.gmeministries.org
www.CysticFibrosisSupportOrg.org

Make certain your quiver is full of hope. This book is purely the Doing
of the Holy One. Be full of life with expectations for tomorrow.

NOTE:
    Cover photo is Dr. Myrna Etheridge's © photo2010, Kingston, New Brunswick,
    Canada.

Books & Music by Dr. Myrna Etheridge

2011 Writing
Watchman on the Wall
Chapters: The Church's WOW Factor, Prayer, Praise & Fasting, This is That,&
Practicing His Presence, Check out: www.gmeministries.org

Newly Released:
Widow—Widower's Helper 2011
Release through www.authorhouse.com POD & eBook,
Divine Exchange, Freedom that Lasts!
Your Trip With Jesus
(1st eBook to replace Your Walk With the LORD)
3 Love Stories of Hope
Ministers in the Web (Co-authored Dr. P. Obadare)

Purpose Driven Marriage (Co-authored Dr. P. Obadare, authorhouse.com)
Marriage Not Manage (Contributing Editor with Dr. Paul Obadare, authorhouse.com)

Making $ense of Your Finances (authorhouse.com)
THE Life Force (Replaced Spring Wind . . . , authorhouse.com)
From Thumb Sucking to Tabret Dancing
Break Forth Into JOY (2nd Edition)
Bringing AID from HIV
How to Keep Your King's Crown of Straight
Momma, What's It Like to Die? Release in /eBook as: Fearing No Evil
To Your GLORY LORD (Music)